About This Book

Title: *From Place to Place*

Step: 4

Word Count: 215

Skills in Focus: Soft c and g

Tricky Words: people, move, across, leave, war, better, travel, some, might, hurt

Ideas For Using This Book

Before Reading:

- **Comprehension:** Look at the title and cover image together. Ask readers to make a prediction about what they might learn in the book. Explain to readers that when people move from one place to another, it is called immigration or migration.
- **Accuracy:** Practice saying the tricky words listed on page 1.
- **Phonemic Awareness:** Tell students they will read words with soft *c* and soft *g* sounds. The letter *c* makes the soft sound /s/ when it is followed by an *e, i,* or *y.* Most of the time, the letter *g* makes the soft sound /j/ when it is followed by an *e, i,* or *y.* Read the title again and ask students which word has a soft *c* sound. Remind readers that the *c* is soft because it is followed by an *e.* Model how to say each sound in the word *place* slowly in isolation. Then, blend the sounds together smoothly to say the whole word. Offer additional examples from the book, such as *huge, barge, face, race, chance,* and *change.*

During Reading:

- Have readers point under each word as they read it.
- **Decoding:** If readers are stuck on a word, help them say each sound and blend the sounds together smoothly. Point out words with soft *c* or soft *g* as they appear.
- **Comprehension:** Invite readers to talk about new things they are learning about immigration and migration while reading. What are they learning that they didn't know before?

After Reading:

Discuss the book. Some ideas for questions:

- What are some ways that you travel from place to place?
- What are some reasons that people might travel to new places?

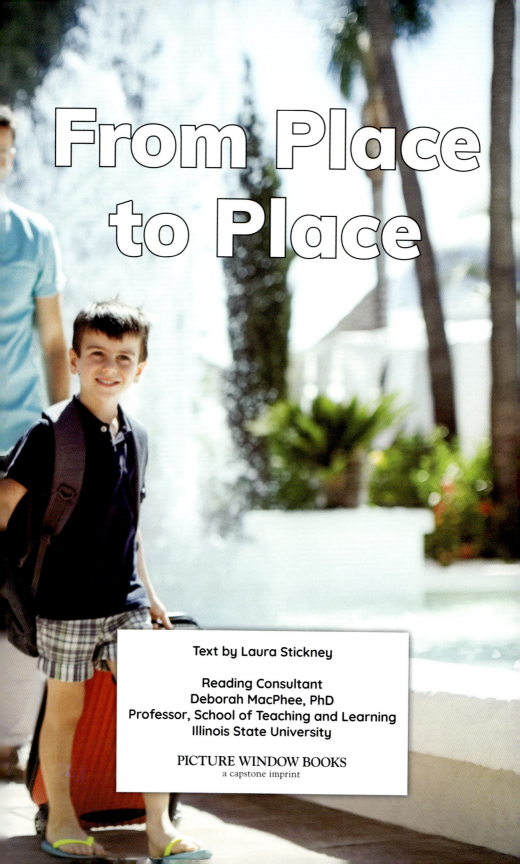

From Place to Place

Text by Laura Stickney

Reading Consultant
Deborah MacPhee, PhD
Professor, School of Teaching and Learning
Illinois State University

PICTURE WINDOW BOOKS
a capstone imprint

Sometimes people move from place to place. This is a big change.

People have been moving from place to place for a long time.

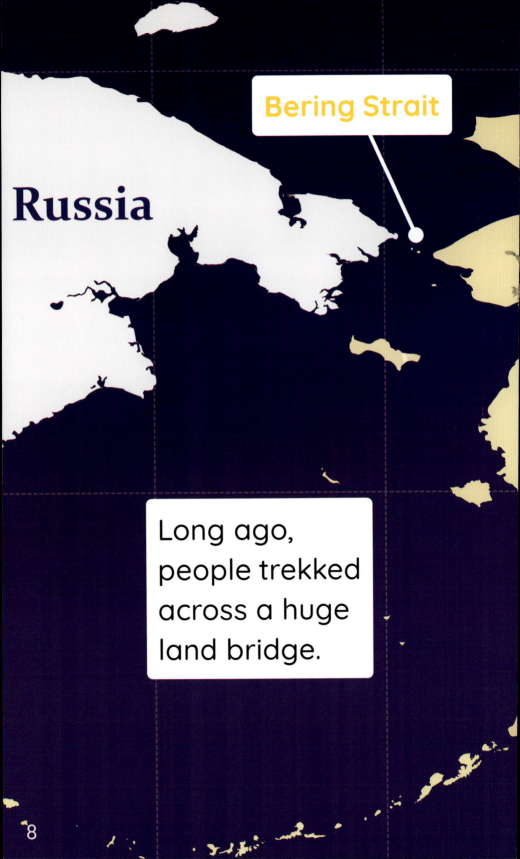

Alaska

Then the land changed. The bridge is not there now.

GULF OF ALASKA

People move across huge, wide spaces.

They go across ridges and dunes.

They drive on bridges in cars.
They go from city to city.

They cross huge seas on ships or rafts.

People of all ages can take trips from place to place.

They leave their homes. It is a chance to find different homes.

Some people go to places to be safe or have a better life.

They want a chance to get jobs with better wages.

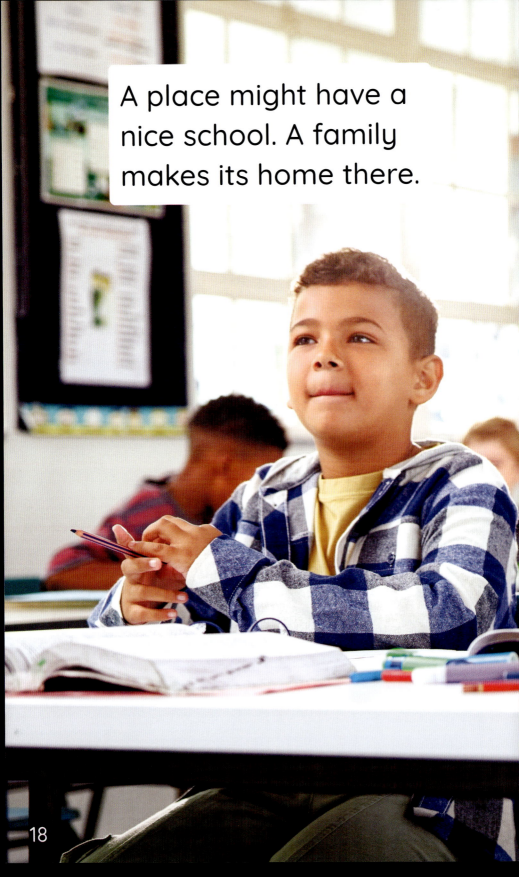

A place might have a nice school. A family makes its home there.

A place can have a war.
Lots of people get hurt.
The place is not safe.

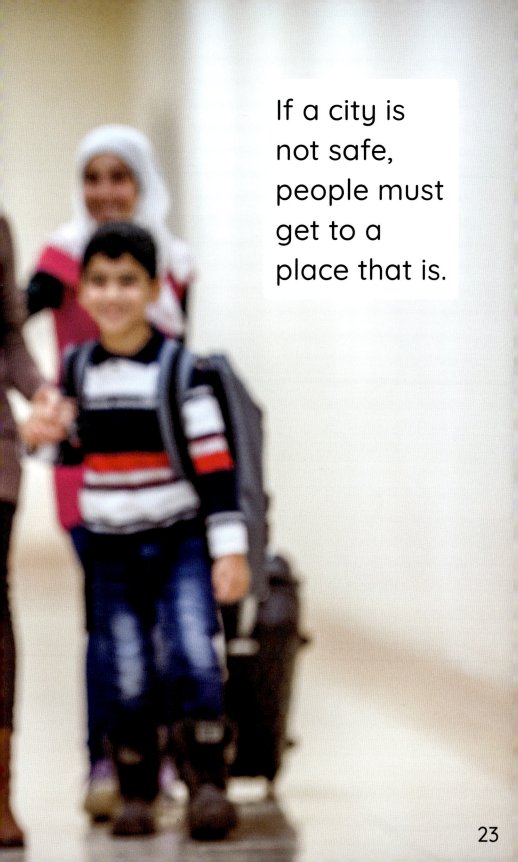

If a city is not safe, people must get to a place that is.

Some people go places for fun trips.

Places have rules about taking trips. They check people who travel to the place.

People in a new place must stand in huge lines.

They need passports with photos of their faces.

They can stay in lodges.

You can go lots of nice places!

More Ideas:

Phonics Activity

Practicing Soft *c* and Soft *g*:
Prepare word cards with story words containing soft and hard *c* and soft and hard *g*. Distribute the cards to the readers. Have students use a marker or highlighter to circle the *c* or *g* in each word. Then have them underline the letter following the *c* or *g* to distinguish whether the *c* or *g* in the word is soft or hard. Students can sort the cards by soft and hard sounds. Words to include:

c words:
- cross
- can
- face
- cut
- nice

g words:
- barge
- huge
- age
- wage
- get
- long
- big

Extended Learning Activity

Story Time:
Ask readers to think about different ways that people move from place to place in the world. Ask them to write a short story about people traveling from one place to another. Have them think about how the people in the story are traveling, where they are going, and why. Challenge readers to use soft *c* and soft *g* words in their story.

Published by Picture Window Books, an imprint of Capstone
1710 Roe Crest Drive, North Mankato, Minnesota 56003
capstonepub.com

Copyright © 2026 by Capstone.
All rights reserved. No part of this publication may be reproduced in whole or in part, or stored in a retrieval system, or transmitted in any form or by any means, electronic, mechanical, photocopying, recording, or otherwise, without written permission of the publisher.

Library of Congress Cataloging-in-Publication Data is available on the Library of Congress website.

ISBN: 9798875227127 (hardback)
ISBN: 9798875230431 (paperback)
ISBN: 9798875230417 (eBook PDF)

Image Credits: iStock: Apiwan Borrikonratchata, 24, Caiaimage/Paul Bradbury, 2–3, 29, FatCamera, 22–23, izusek, 14, Maksims Grigorjevs, 28, Michael Derrer Fuchs, 16–17, monkeybusinessimages, 1, 25, MoreISO, 10–11, 32, xavierarnau, cover; Shutterstock: ArtemisDiana, 8–9, Everett Collection, 6–7, Iv-olga, 12, kibri_ho, 20–21, Monkey Business Images, 15, Netfalls Remy Musser, 13, PeopleImages.com/Yuri A, 26–27, Rido, 18–19, Tomsickova Tatyana, 4–5, Yaroslav Astakhov, 30

Printed and bound in China. 6274